A CITY THROUGH TIME

ILLUSTRATION: STEVE NOON

London, New York,
Melbourne, Munich, and Delhi

Senior Art Editor Sheila Collins
Editor Matilda Gollon
Designer Katie Knutton
Managing Editor Linda Esposito
Managing Art Editor Diane Peyton Jones
Category Publisher Laura Buller
Publishing Director Jonathan Metcalf
Associate Publishing Director Liz Wheeler
Art Director Phil Ormerod
Production Editor Nikoleta Parasaki
Senior Production Controller Sophie Argyris
Jacket Designer Laura Brim
Jacket Editor Manisha Majithia

DK India
Design Intern Shreya Sadhan
Art Editor Shipra Jain, Supriya Mahajan
Senior Art Editor Anjana Nair
Managing Art Editor Arunesh Talapatra
DTP Designer Anita Yadav
DTP Manager Balwant Singh
Picture Researcher Sakshi Saluja
Picture Researcher Manager Taiyaba Khatoon

First published in Great Britain in 2013 by
Dorling Kindersley Limited,
80 Strand, London WC2R 0RL

10 9 8 7 6 5 4 3
011–187513–03/13

A CIP catalogue record for this book is available from the British Library.

ISBN: 978-1-4093-6453-5

Printed and bound by
Leo, China

Discover more at
www.dk.com

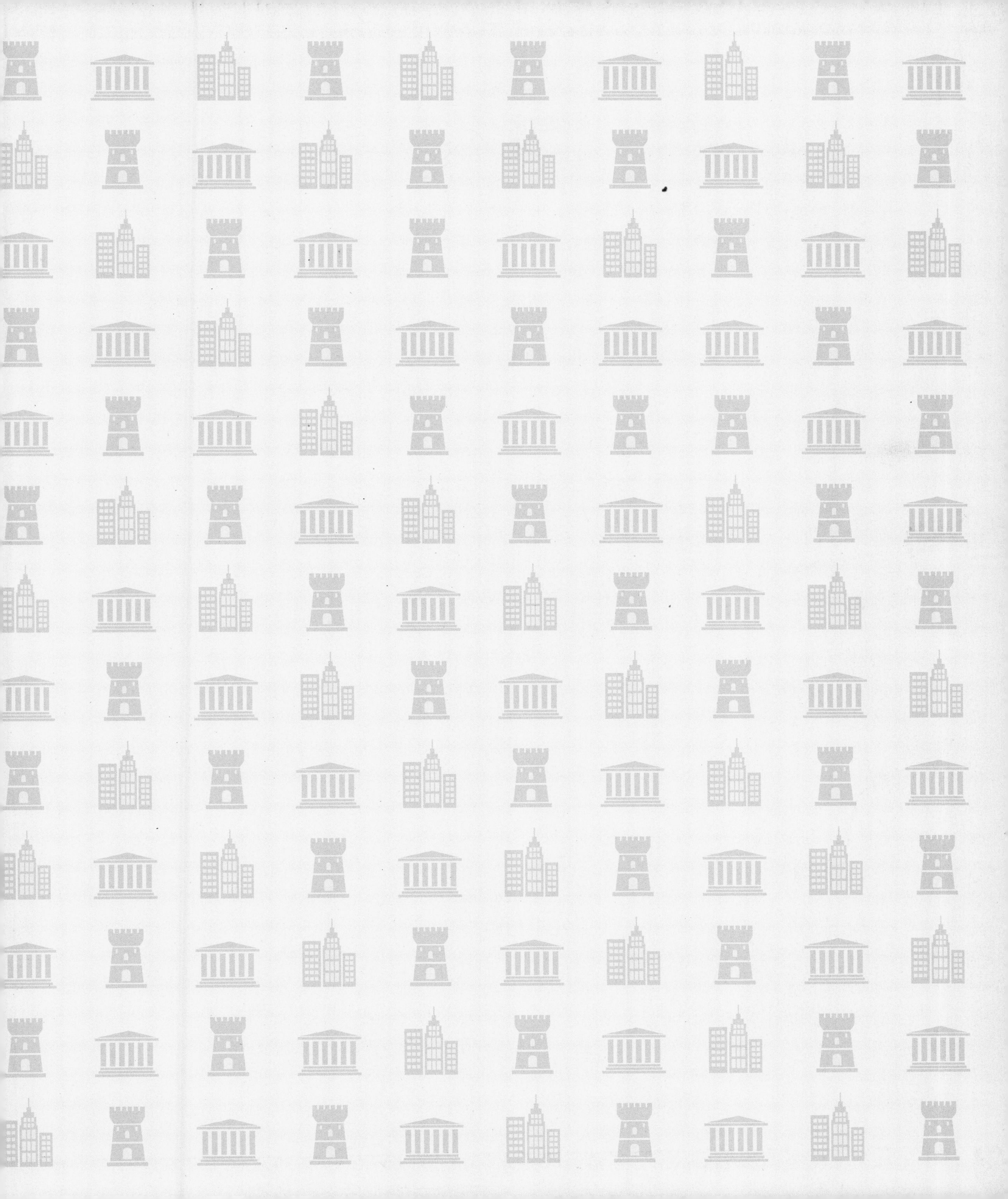

CONTENTS

THE STORY OF A CITY

Imagine a huge city. Its buildings light up the night sky. Beyond the city centre are factories and motorways, airports and docks. Tall cranes rise into the sky. Sometimes builders dig up ancient remains, such as Stone Age arrowheads or Roman coins. These show that people have lived here for thousands of years. Some very old buildings still stand. The cathedral has loomed above the rooftops since medieval times.

Why did people settle here so long ago, at the mouth of a river on the Mediterranean coast? First, there was fresh drinking water. Fish could be caught in the sea. Later, people found that wheat grew well in the soil. There was stone and timber for building. This was a good place for traders to meet, too. Many sailed here from distant lands. The city grew rich and its rulers became very powerful.

However much the city changed, the people who lived there had the same basic needs as those first settlers. They wanted fresh water, food, and shelter. They wanted to lead healthy and happy lives. They wanted work, trade, and travel by land and sea. They wanted a city that was organized and well run. If we could meet our ancestors, we would probably discover that they were very like ourselves.

STONE AGE HUNTERS
(AROUND 14,000 YEARS AGO)

A roaming band of hunters spends each winter on the hill. They sleep in caves and paint pictures on rocks. They fish in the river and make weapons of sharp flints and hard wood. They wear cloaks of animal skin and bone necklaces. Warriors paint their faces with red clay.

A CAMP BY THE RIVER
(AROUND 8,000 YEARS AGO)

The hunters spread out along the river banks. They shoot ducks using arrows tipped with tiny but deadly flints. The hunters have set up camp with tents made of deerskin and timber poles. Soon they will leave and search for new hunting grounds.

THE FIRST FARMERS
(AROUND 6,000 YEARS AGO)

Now there are stone, timber, and thatch huts on the hillside all year round. This is a farming village. People still hunt, but they no longer need to move in search of food. The harvest gives them enough food for the whole year.

TOMBS TO HONOUR THE DEAD
(AROUND 5,000 YEARS AGO)

Slabs of rock are broken off the cliffs by the river. They are chipped into shape and hauled away with ropes. The chief of the tribe is building a tomb of earth and stone. He will be laid there when he dies. Everyone who sees the tomb will honour his memory.

THE METALWORKERS
(AROUND 4,500 YEARS AGO)

The villagers have learned to mine copper and to separate it from the rock by heat. They pour the molten metal into moulds and make it into weapons and jewellery. These can be exchanged with other tribes in return for food and other goods.

TRADERS FROM THE SEA
(AROUND 3,000 YEARS AGO)

Merchant ships are drawn up on the beach below the settlement. The sailors are Phoenicians and Cretans, from far to the east. They trade in glass beads, cloth, timber, and wine from across the sea. Some of these foreign traders settle here.

THE GREEK COLONY (550 BCE)

Greek settlers built this city at the mouth of a river a hundred years ago. Merchants still sail from Greece to trade in the market, but so do Phoenicians from Syria, Etruscans from Italy, and Celts from the lands beyond the hills. They buy jars of the best Greek wine. The colony grows wheat and olives, and there are plenty of fish in the sea. Sometimes the colonists attack passing ships and steal their cargoes.

TYRANT

A tyrant rules the city. He seized power from the aristocracy, who now despise him.

PHILOSOPHER

This philosopher wants to find out why things exist and what they are made of.

GIRL

A girl plucks the strings of a lyre. She is playing at a banquet.

CHILDREN

As soon as they have finished lessons with their tutor, the children run out to play.

WHO'S WHO?

Here are some of the people you might meet in the Greek colony.

MOTHER
A mother shows her daughters how to weave a woollen blanket on an upright loom.

SLAVE
A slave carries water from the well. She is owned by her master and doesn't get paid.

MERCHANT
A merchant carries greens, leeks, and onions to market on the back of his donkey.

POTTER
The potter shapes wet clay with his fingers. He makes cups, jugs, storage jars, and bowls.

BRIDE
This bride is 18 years old. She is trying on a veil in preparation for her wedding day.

ATHLETE
This athlete is famous. He travelled all the way to Greece for the Olympic Games.

HOPLITE
This hoplite is named after his round shield, the hoplon. He fights with a spear and sword.

FISHERMAN
A fisherman walks back from the seashore. His catch should fetch a good price at market.

THE TEMPLE (550 BCE)

Today there is a harvest festival, to honour the goddess Demeter. An excited procession winds up the hill to the new temple. Oxen bellow as they are led to be killed at the altar. This sacrifice will bring the city good fortune. The Greeks worship many gods and goddesses. Every child knows the old tales about the gods. The stories are exciting, for the gods are always quarrelling, playing tricks, or falling in love.

ALTAR AND TEMPLE

Public ceremonies take place at the altar outside the temple. Private worship may take place in the holiest part of the temple, the inner sanctuary. It is a large dark hall, lit by flickering flames. There is a massive statue of the goddess Demeter, holding fruit as a symbol of the harvest.

GREEK GODS

The Greeks believe that the gods and goddesses watch over them. The sailor prays to Poseidon for calm seas. The hunter asks Artemis to guide his spear.

ZEUS

Zeus is father of the gods. He rules Earth from Mount Olympus. If angry, he hurls down lightning and thunderbolts.

ATHENA

Athena, daughter of Zeus, is goddess of battle and wisdom. She protects olive groves and many cities in the Greek world.

HOLY MEN

Priests are chosen from the most important families in the colony. They make sure that all the rituals and ceremonies are followed properly.

TEMPLE DECORATION

The temple used to be made of wood but was rebuilt in marble. It is decorated with statues and paintings of gods, humans, animals, and strange beasts.

GIFTS FOR THE GODS

Animals sacrificed to the gods include oxen, sheep, and cockerels. Another way to please the gods is to give money to the temple priests.

POSEIDON

Poseidon, old and powerful, is the brother of Zeus. He is god of the sea, shaker of the Earth, and the lord of horses.

ARTEMIS

Artemis, another daughter of Zeus, is the goddess of wild animals and hunting. She is armed with a bow and arrows.

DEMETER

Demeter is goddess of grain, the seasons, fertility, and death. She is worshipped wherever the Greeks have settled.

CITIZENS OF ROME (120 CE)

Romans are now in control of the city. The Roman empire stretches across most of Europe and to parts of Africa and Asia. The city now has straight, paved roads, and soldiers patrol the city walls. In the temple, the Romans worship the same gods as the Greeks, but they call them different names. The citizens relax at the public baths and are entertained in the amphitheatre. Today a famous gladiator is fighting in the ring.

PATRON
The patron is a wealthy and powerful man who protects the client. The patron wants to be a politician.

CLIENT
The client supports the patron's business deals and political schemes. He is given money in return.

MATRON
This rich married woman has four children. She runs her own small business, and rents out some shops.

LABOURER
This labourer is employed by the town council to repair roads and bridges.

WHO'S WHO?

Here are some of the people you might meet in the Roman city.

DRAPER

A draper sells rolls of woollen or linen cloth. Cotton is sometimes imported from Egypt.

OLD MAN

An old man hurries home to his farm. He has been selling honey in town.

SLAVES

Slaves work as servants or labourers. In the end, a lucky few might be given their freedom.

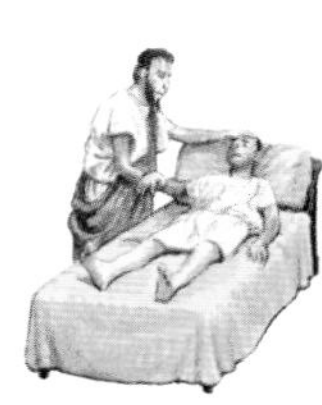

DOCTOR

The doctor is checking a sick man's symptoms to see what is wrong with him.

LEGIONARY

The legionary belongs to an army unit called a legion. He might have to serve anywhere in the empire.

GLADIATOR

This gladiator was once a criminal. He was let off so that he could fight in the amphitheatre.

YOUNG WOMAN

A young woman practises the cithara, a musical instrument first used in Greece.

ACTOR

The actor wears a sad mask for tragedies and a happy mask for comedies.

THE PUBLIC BATHS (120 CE)

The bathhouse is busy today. Slaves hurry through the steam, carrying fresh towels. Is it to be the hot room or the cold room? The warm bath or the cold plunge? A massage or a workout? Everyone loves the baths. Businessmen swap stories and mop their brows. Soldiers quarrel and play dice. Tomorrow it is the women's turn. They laugh and chat as they do their sewing. Visiting the baths is part of the Roman way of life.

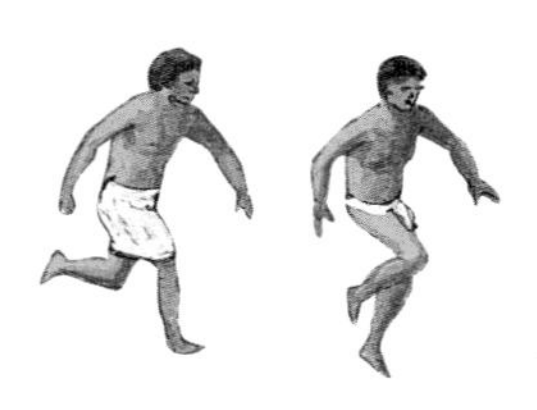

EXERCISE

Bathers can start with some exercise outside in the yard. They run, wrestle, or lift weights.

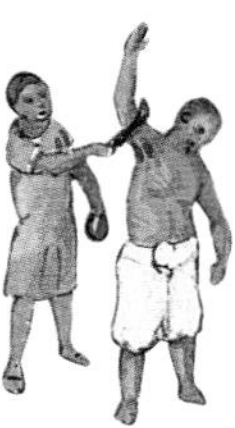

OIL AND STRIGILS

To wash, the Romans rub oil into their skin, then scrape it off with a blade called a strigil. Away comes all the grime, too!

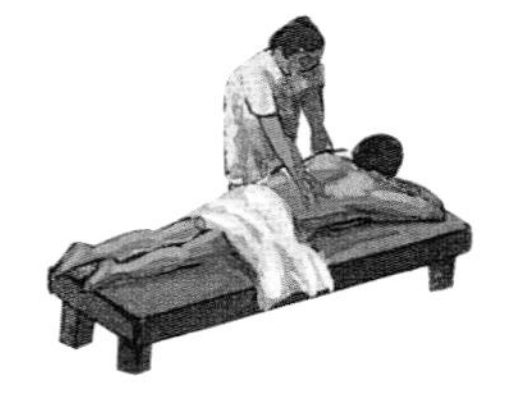

MASSAGE

Bathers can also relax with a massage. Scented olive oils are rubbed into their skin to make them smell nice.

BATHING IN STYLE

The walls of the bathhouse are covered in paintings and the floors are decorated with mosaics. These are pictures or patterns made out of fragments of coloured stone, pottery, or glass.

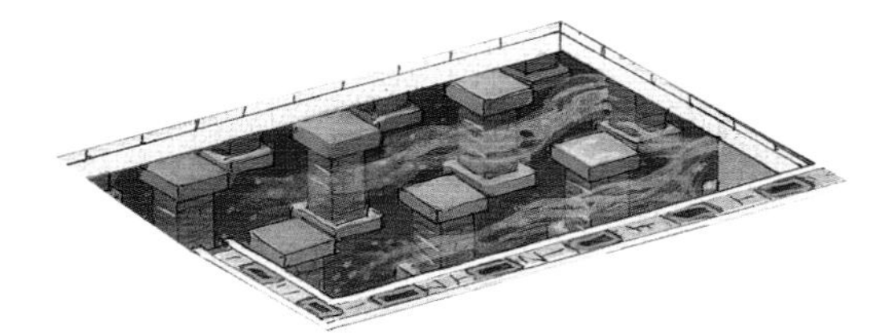

CENTRAL HEATING

Hot air from a big furnace passes through ducts under the floor and behind the walls. The floors get so hot in the warmer rooms that bathers wear sandals to protect their feet.

WATER SUPPLY

Water for the baths comes from springs in the hills. It is carried to the city along aqueducts. These might be channels or pipes, above or below ground. Some run alongside the road. Arches support an aqueduct if it has to cross a valley.

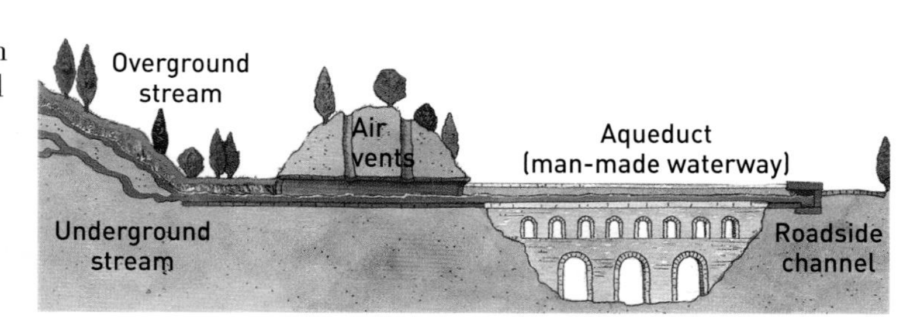

RESERVOIR

The aqueduct water flows into a big reservoir (supply tank). It takes a lot of water to fill the baths and flush away waste. Instead of toilet paper, people use sponges on sticks, which they wash clean after use. Waste water flows into the sewer.

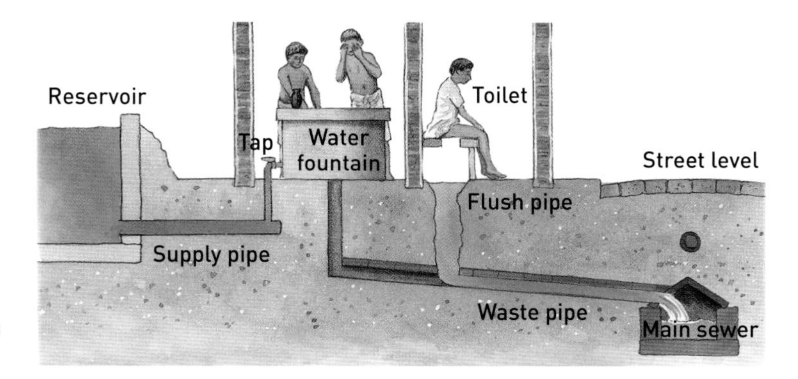

HOT WATER

The hot water tank is heated by a duct that carries hot air rising from the furnace. Currents of hot water from this heated tank enter the bath. As they cool, they sink and return to the tank, where they are heated again.

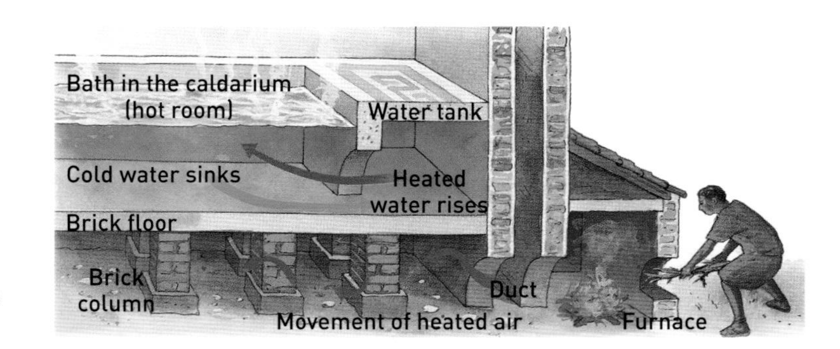

HAVING A DIP

The hot room offers a relaxing soak in the small pool. Finally, bathers freshen up with a cold dip.

CATCHING UP

The bathhouse is an important social meeting place. Bathers chat about business and politics.

MALE BATHING TIME

Mixed bathing is not allowed. Male and female bathing sessions are at different times or in separate areas.

THE MEDIEVAL CITY (1250)

A massive castle now towers over the city. It belongs to the count, one of the most powerful men in the land. A new cathedral is rising above the rooftops, too, a symbol of the Church's power and wealth. The city has been Christian now for more than 900 years. Although the city streets are narrow and dirty, the market square is busy and prosperous – just look at the fine town hall and merchants' houses.

POPE
The Pope is far away in Rome. He is head of the Church and more powerful than the king.

BISHOP
The bishop is the regional Church leader, and very proud of his splendid new cathedral.

MONKS AND NUNS
Monks and nuns follow a life of prayer. Some teach and some care for the sick.

LAWYER
This lawyer studied at the University of Bologna, in Italy. His dealings have made him wealthy.

WHO'S WHO?

Here are some of the people you might meet in the medieval city.

KING

The king rules over all the land. Even the count must obey him, although they often quarrel.

COUNT

The count governs the whole region. He is very rich. Knights swear loyalty to him.

CRUSADER KNIGHT

The crusader is riding to the Holy Land to fight religious wars. He is blessed by the bishop before he goes.

FOOT SOLDIERS

Foot soldiers are in the service of the knights and nobles. They guard the count's castle.

BLACKSMITH

A blacksmith shoes horses and mends tools and weapons at his forge. It is thirsty work!

MERCHANTS

Merchants buy and sell goods in the marketplace. Some of them make more money than the nobles.

FARM WORKERS

Farm workers plough the count's land. They are not allowed to leave or work for anyone else.

CITY WORKERS

City workers include builders, carpenters, servants, washerwomen, and sewage shovellers.

THE CASTLE (1250)

A castle has stood here for 300 years now. At first it was built of timber, but that was soon destroyed. Gradually, it was rebuilt in stone and today the castle walls extend to surround the whole city. Knights ride out from here to fight the count's enemies. Castle officials ride through the count's lands, collecting taxes. Nobody likes them! City and country folk alike must supply the castle with labour or food.

BECOMING A KNIGHT

Being a knight is expensive, so most candidates come from noble or wealthy families. It can then take up to 12 years to become a knight.

YOUNG BOY

A young boy becomes a page in a noble's castle. He does chores and is taught good manners.

PAGE

He also learns how to ride a horse well and how to fight using practice weapons.

SQUIRE

The page becomes a squire to a knight. He helps his master with his armour.

IN THE GARDEN

Herbs are grown in the garden to make medicines. Birds of prey, which are used for hunting, are also kept here in the mews.

GOOD SHOT!

During a siege, the castle's soldiers can fire arrows at the enemy through gaps in the walls called crenels.

A NOBLE LIFE

The castle is a home as well as a stronghold. The count and his family live safely in the towers.

INTO BATTLE

The squire soon masters his own use of weapons and accompanies the knight into battle.

CEREMONY

After making vows to God and oaths of loyalty to his lord, he is "knighted" by a noble or the king himself.

FAMILY HONOUR

The knight seeks glory in battle, wearing his family coat of arms. He must also make a good marriage and win powerful friends.

PALACES AND FOUNTAINS (1650)

Hooves clatter and cartwheels rumble over the cobblestones. Street sellers call out their wares: "Come buy!" Around the tavern, rowdy musketeers are singing out of tune. Rats scamper along the quays by the river and wriggle through attics and gutters. In the city square, fashionable ladies and gentlemen are bowing and curtseying to each other. The count's grand palace is built beside the ruins of the old castle, on the hill.

FOOTMAN

The footman is a servant who opens the doors of coaches, ushers in guests, and serves at the dining table.

ACTRESS

This actress appears in comedies at the theatre. She is very popular with everyone in the city.

PRIEST AND NUN

The priest and nun comfort the sick. The city is a centre of the Catholic faith, with many new churches.

BEGGAR

A beggar demands money in the street. He lost an eye and a leg in the wars.

WHO'S WHO?

Here are some of the people you might meet in the city in the 17th century.

MUSKETEER

The musketeer is armed with a gun called a musket. He is meant to keep order, but often gets into brawls.

PEDLAR

The pedlar sells lots of things in the street – from pots and pans to ribbons and toys.

INNKEEPER

The innkeeper is kept very busy, even though people say he waters down the wine.

DENTIST

The dentist is pulling out a man's rotten tooth! He often works as a surgeon too.

COUNT AND COUNTESS

The count and countess are the city's wealthiest couple. They spend most of their time away at the royal court.

SAILOR

The sailor has shipped brandy to northern Europe and brought back sugar from the West Indies.

CUTPURSE

A cutpurse darts among the crowds. He stealthily picks people's pockets.

GOOSE GIRL

A goose girl brings her flock to market in the city and sells the birds for food.

THE TOWN HALL (1650)

The harvest this year was a poor one. Grain is scarce, so flour and bread have become very expensive. Only the rich can afford them. Hungry protestors gather at the gates of the town hall. They want food for their families. A clerk in the tax office drops his quill pen in panic, spilling ink. "Call out the Guard!" he bellows. "Summon the Grand Council!" yells another.

COOKING UP A FEAST

A banquet is being prepared for members of the Grand Council. Servants lay out silver plates. Cooks shout out orders in the steamy kitchen.

EMERGENCY MEETING

The Grand Council agree that they will refuse to give in to the mob. An official flings open a window. "Go away or we will shoot you down!"

INSIDE CITY HALL

The city is run from this grand public building. Inside, clerks tally up the taxes, officials meet, valuables are locked away, and prisoners are put on trial. The building is protected by guards.

PROTESTERS

People cannot afford to pay taxes, but the king needs money to pay for his foreign wars. Tax collectors go around the city. They bully people and threaten them with jail if they refuse to pay up.

ON TRIAL

Prisoners are held in the lockup. One stands in the courtroom, accused of highway robbery.

STRIKING A POSE

The commander of the guard is having his portrait painted. When the trouble starts, he runs downstairs with his sword.

ARM YOURSELVES

Weapons are kept in the armoury, but gunpowder is stored in the castle ruins because of the risk of fire.

THE INDUSTRIAL PORT (1880)

Factory chimneys rise above the rooftops. Trains clank and hiss at the station, belching out smoke. More than two million people live here now. The city's suburbs stretch all the way to the new docks at the river mouth. There, big ships bring sugar, cotton, hardwoods, coffee, and tea from distant lands. The city's water supply is still poor, but new drains and sewers are being built and there is a new hospital.

INDUSTRIALIST

The industrialist has made a fortune from his factories. He owns a lot of land and buildings.

LADY

This lady follows the latest Paris fashions. She is married to a wealthy industrialist.

TEXTILE WORKER

The textile worker moved to the city to find factory work. Cloth-making is a growing industry.

NANNY

The nanny wheels a perambulator or "pram". She works for a family that has many children.

WHO'S WHO?

Here are some of the people you might meet in the industrial city.

FLOWER SELLER

This woman sells colourful flowers to brighten up people's clothes and homes.

PAPER BOY

A newspaper boy calls out the latest headline: "Scandal at the town hall! Read all about it!"

POLICEMAN

The policeman wears a smart uniform. He blows his whistle if he spots trouble.

PHOTOGRAPHER

The photographer is taking a photograph of the grocer. Lots of people have come to watch.

GROCER

The grocer wears a long white apron. His fruit and vegetables are neatly stacked and displayed.

CAB DRIVER

The cab driver knows every street in the city and its suburbs. His horse is smartly groomed.

SOLDIER

The soldier is going to the railway station. He is being sent to serve in an overseas colony.

LAMPLIGHTER

The lamplighter does his rounds each evening. He must light every gas lamp in the street.

THE RAILWAY STATION (1880)

Welcome to the grand terminal of the Southern European Railway Company. It is one of the most important buildings in the city. An express train has just pulled in, puffing and steaming. Brakes squeal. Carriage doors fly open and porters struggle with heavy luggage. The railway line stretches all the way to Madrid, Paris, or Rome. Other trains are local, bringing in workers from the suburbs.

WHERE TO, SIR?

Horse-drawn cabs pick up passengers. Some go to the Grand Hotel, others to a new exhibition.

PASSENGERS

Businessmen, soldiers off to war, and girls in the latest Paris fashions all travel by train.

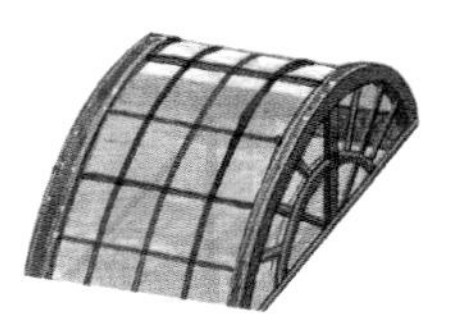

IRON AND GLASS

Iron pillars and arches hold up the glass roofs, which cover the platforms and shelter the pavement.

THE GOODS YARD

Freight is being unloaded in the goods yard. All sorts of things are transported by train. Workers in the goods yard handle coal, sand, gravel, cables, machines, cattle, fish, grain, and milk.

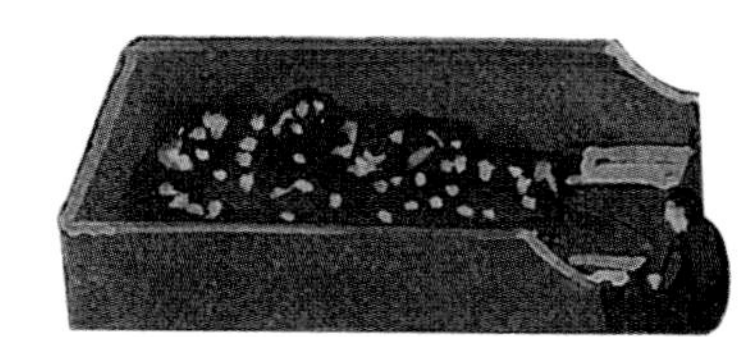

IN THE SIDINGS

Bang! Clank! Trains are shunted into the sidings. Workers shovel coal and fill up the water on the steam engines. Points move the locomotives from one track to another.

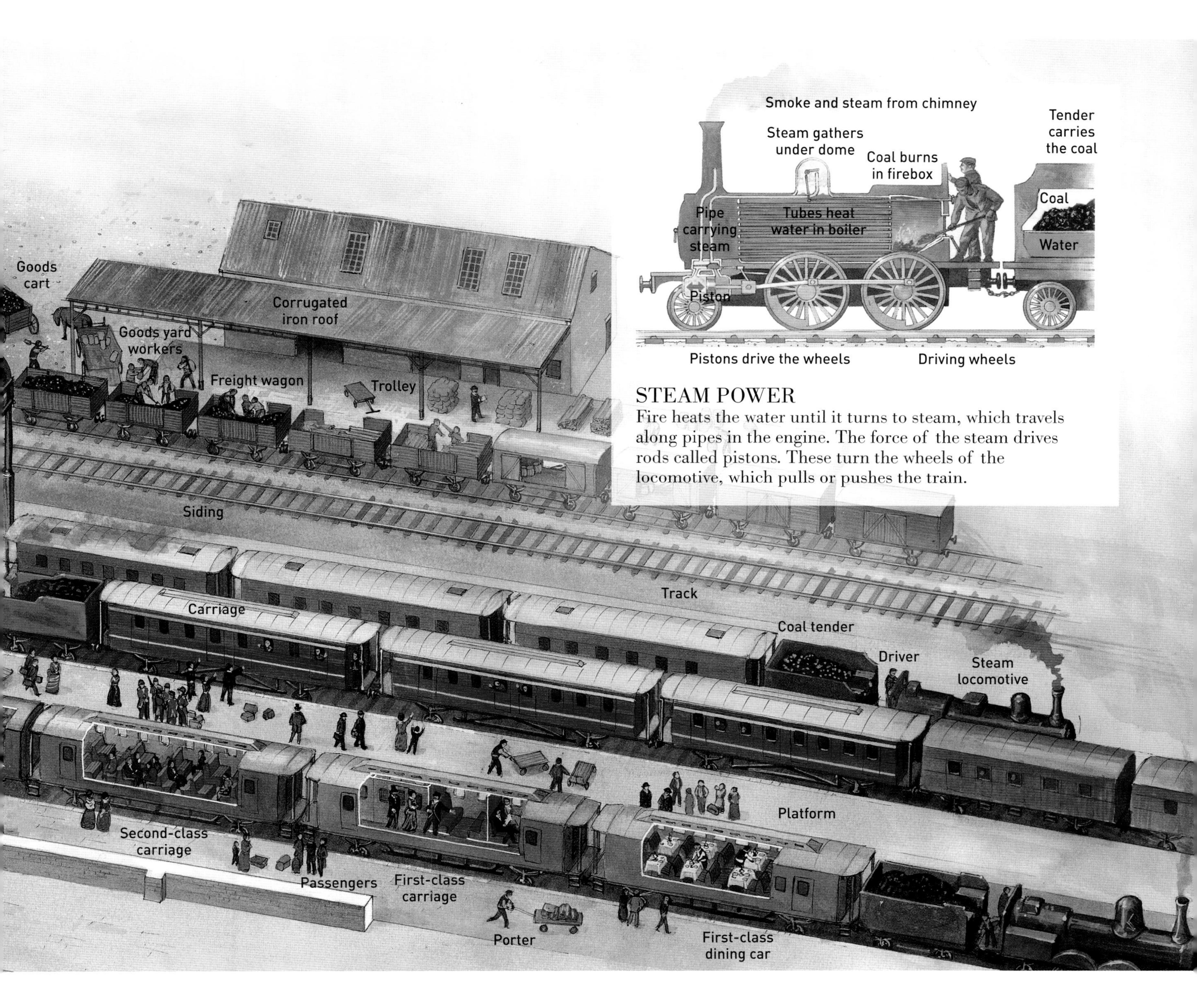

STEAM POWER

Fire heats the water until it turns to steam, which travels along pipes in the engine. The force of the steam drives rods called pistons. These turn the wheels of the locomotive, which pulls or pushes the train.

MAIL VAN

The postal service uses the railway to transport sacks of letters from one city to another.

SECOND CLASS

Ordinary people can afford to travel by train in the lower-class carriages.

FIRST CLASS

Wealthy people travel in luxurious carriages. They can even have a meal on board in the dining car.

STEEL AND GLASS (TODAY)

The streets light up as it gets dark. There are car headlights, traffic lights, glowing shop signs, and flashing advertisements. Office workers switch off their computers and hurry home. People crowd into underground railway stations, shopping malls, cinemas, and parks. Everyone seems to be in a hurry. The Old Town on the hill is lit up as well. It is now just part of a huge, modern city.

WAITER

The waiter balances drinks on his tray and can carry several plates of hot food at once.

COMMUTER

The commuter works at a bank. She travels in from the suburbs by underground railway.

TV CREW

The TV crew report on news stories and interview people around the city.

PARAMEDIC

The paramedic travels in an ambulance. She is trained to save lives if there is a bad accident.

WHO'S WHO?

Here are some of the people you might meet in the modern city.

GYM INSTRUCTOR

The gym instructor helps keep office workers fit. They visit the gym after work to do exercises.

COURIER

The motorcycle courier darts through the traffic, delivering urgent packages.

BUILDER

The construction worker wears a hard hat on the building site.

SWEEPER

The road sweeper picks up rubbish, such as drink cans, sweet wrappers, and takeaway food cartons.

BUSKER

The busker sings songs to passers-by. If they like his music, they throw coins into his hat.

CYCLIST

The cyclist zips past the cars and gets to do some exercise on his commute to work.

TOURIST

This tourist is queueing up to take a boat trip along the river. She plans to take some photographs.

POLICE OFFICER

This police offiicer controls the traffic. She tries to keep the cars moving, preventing traffic jams.

HIGH-RISE (TODAY)

The new City Tower has just opened. Its strong foundations of steel and concrete are pinned into the ancient bedrock beneath the city. This tall building contains offices, shops, a hotel, a cinema, and a gymnasium – it is like a city in miniature. Take a lift to the rooftop restaurant, and the whole city is spread out below. Look to the north and you can see the Old Town, where the story of the city began.

SAVING ENERGY

Insulation, such as living tiles of green grass on the roof, prevent heat being lost. Solar panels collect energy from the Sun. They trap heat and use it to warm water supplies.

DINING IN THE SKY

The rooftop restaurant has one of the best views in the entire city. It serves locally produced food.

WORKING OUT

Office workers, who spend all day sitting at a computer, come to the gymnasium on the ninth floor to get fit.

OFFICES

At the advertising agency people think up clever ways to sell cars, CDs, and all sorts of other products.

Solar panels
Grass panels
Bar
Roof terrace
Café
Waiter
Chef
Restaurant
Restaurant kitchens
Gym
Instructor
Weights
Cycle machines
Rowing machines
Running machines
Boardroom
Files
Toilets
Manager
Secretary
Air-conditioning vents
Computers
Fire-extinguishing sprinklers
Advertising agency offices
Public art
Office lobby
Express lift
Internal lifts
Office reception
Air-conditioning external vents

GOING UP!

High-rises depend on lifts. An express lift whizzes up the outside of the building to the restaurant. The main lifts are on the inside of the building.

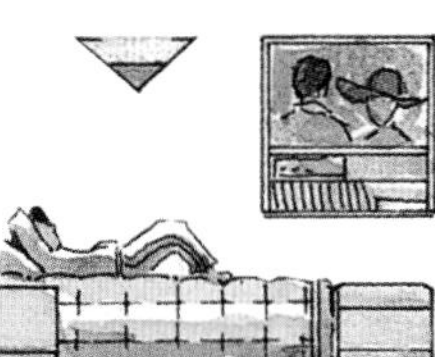

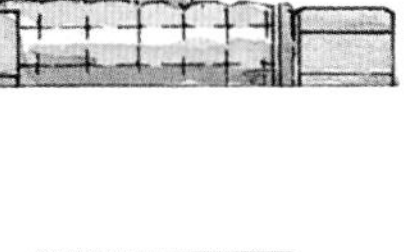

STYLISH HOTEL

Visitors come to the city for business or to see the old cathedral. Some of them stay at this luxury hotel.

LEISURE

Boutiques sell expensive clothes, handbags, jewellery, and shoes. The mini cinema shows the latest films from around the world.

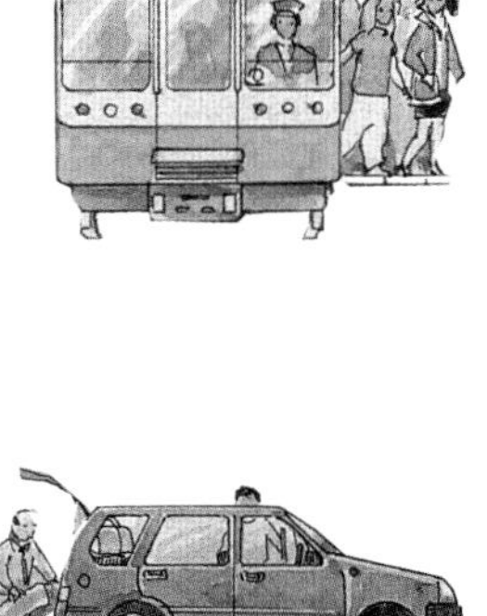

UNDERGROUND

A network of underground railway lines runs under the city. The trains are powered by electricity. Passengers reach street level by escalators.

CAR PARKS

This building has its own underground car park. There are few spaces to park on the street in the city.

SERVICING THE BUILDING

The high-rise is connected to city-wide supplies of electricity, water, and gas. The building depends on these for its lighting, lifts, computer systems, telephones, heating, air conditioning, and kitchens.

ARCHITECTURE THROUGH TIME

Greek

Acropolis: A rocky area of high ground at the centre of most Greek cities. It was easy to defend and was often the site of forts and temples.

Agora: The city centre, made up of a busy marketplace and public buildings.

Colony: A settlement built in another land. The Greeks built colonies throughout their history.

Column: A stone pillar designed to support a roof.

Gymnasium: An area for men and boys to exercise and play sport. It was also a place for meeting and discussion.

Pediment: A triangular gable or roof end, often decorated with painted sculptures.

Stoa: A building with columns and walkways, used as a meeting place.

Theatre: An open-air arena with rows of stone benches, arranged in a half-circle and set into a hillside. Greek drama was performed here.

Temple with columns

Roman

Amphitheatre: An oval or circular building with seats for spectators. In the centre was an arena (area of sand) where shows were staged.

Inside an amphitheatre

Arches and domes: Strong curved structures that support themselves. Engineers used them in buildings and bridges.

Basilica: A public building, used to conduct law and commerce.

Cloacae: Drains and sewers built in many towns to carry waste and dirty water into the nearest river.

Domus: A house, often designed around an open atrium (courtyard).

Forum: An open square at the centre of a Roman town. It was a public meeting place and surrounded by shops, temples, and public buildings.

Insula: An "island" or block of housing within the streets of a Roman town. In large cities, it might be taken up by a tall, crowded apartment block.

Villa: A large, grand home built outside the town by a wealthy Roman.

Medieval

Battlements: The upper walls of a castle or city defences. They were used as a platform for fighting and as a shield.

Cathedral: The most important Christian church in a region, and often the largest and most splendid.

City walls: Thick stone walls surrounded the whole city during medieval times. They were used to defend the city from attack. The gates were closed at night.

Crenels: Gaps in battlement walls. Arrows could be fired through the crenels, or rocks could be dropped onto the enemy below.

Medieval cathedral

Loops: Narrow slits in castle and city walls, used for firing arrows at the enemy.

Merlons: Raised sections of battlements. They provided cover from attack.

Monastery: A building where monks lived and worshipped. Many medieval monasteries also served as libraries, schools, or hospitals.

17th century

Coats of arms: Badges used by noble families since medieval times. Coats of arms of families, guilds, traders and craftspeople, and cities were often carved into stone walls or displayed on flags, banners, and tapestries.

Palace and garden

Gardens: In the 1600s, gardens were laid out around palaces, public buildings, and squares. They included low hedges and paths arranged in intricate patterns, as well as statues and fountains.

Inn: A building that offered food, drink, and a bed for people, and stabling for horses. Inns were also places to hire horses or to start a journey by horse-drawn coach.

Palace: A grand house with many rooms, built for noble or royal families. It was not fortified against attack.

Theatre: An enclosed public building for performances. Plays took place on a stage in front of painted scenery. Theatres might be closed during times of plague, or if the king did not like the play.

19th century

Botanical gardens: Gardens whose gardeners collected plants for scientific study. Their new greenhouses were made of cast iron and glass.

Factories: Large brick buildings with tall, smoking chimneys. Factories and mills contained machinery that produced steel, glass, cloth, and pottery on a large scale.

Hospitals: New hospitals were light and airy. Doctors and nurses learned to keep wards clean and free of germs.

Prisons: New prisons were built with cells and high walls. They were cleaner and less damp than dungeons.

Suspension bridge

Sewers: Brick tunnels for carrying sewage, built under streets to replace open drains and improve public health.

Suspension bridge: A bridge whose roadway is supported by hanging chains or cables.

Today

Escalators: Moving staircases in large stores, shopping malls, airports, and underground railways.

High-rise buildings: Tall buildings built around steel frames. Their foundations are embedded deep in rock.

Lifts: Capsules that transport people up and down tall buildings. Lifts were essential for the development of skyscrapers.

Pedestrian zone: An area in a city centre with streets given over to walkers, not cars.

Shopping mall: A building where people can visit many shops at different levels.

Underground car park: A place to leave cars below street level, built to create more space in crowded cities.

Telecommunication masts: Aerials used to relay radio, television, and phone signals.

Shopping mall

TECHNOLOGY THROUGH TIME

Greek

Coins: Greeks were making coins and trading with them from 595 BCE. A smith placed a disc of hot metal on a raised metal pattern called a die. He then hammered the disc to create a patterned coin.

Metalwork: Greeks made bronze from about 2900 BCE. They used iron from about 1050 BCE for swords, spears, axe-heads, knives, and hammers.

Pottery: The Greeks shaped clay pots on a wheel and heated them in an oven at about 540°C (1,000°F). They often painted scenes of gods and goddesses, or of everyday life on the pots.

Transport: The wealthy used horses for travel. The poor used mules and donkeys. Oxen hauled wagons. Fast chariots were used for racing, but were no longer popular in battle.

Triremes: Greek warships made of timber, with a crew of 200. They were powered by three banks of oars on each side.

Greek metalworkers

Roman

Aqueduct: A stone channel or pipe used to carry water.

Roman aqueduct

Cement: A substance made of lime and sand. It has been used since 300 BCE as a kind of glue for binding together stonework.

Concrete: A mixture of lime and ground rock, invented in about 55 BCE. It was cheaper and often stronger than stone.

Glass: The Romans were great glass makers. They knew how to blow hot glass into shapes through a long tube. They made bottles, jugs, and bowls.

Hypocaust: A central heating system powered by a furnace. Hot air from the furnace passed under the floors and behind the walls.

Iron: The most important metal for the Romans. Smiths hammered out tools, weapons, armour, pots, and pans.

Pottery: The Romans had large pottery factories wherever there were good supplies of clay. There were big centres of production in Italy, France, and Germany.

Roads: The Romans built a road system across Europe. The roads were straight, well drained, and built on strong foundations. They were paved with stone slabs, gravel, or stone chippings.

Medieval

Candles: Candles made from animal fat had been used for lighting since Greek times. In medieval times, fine candles were made from beeswax. Some candles were marked in stages to show the time they took to burn. These were an early sort of clock.

Milling: The flour for the city's bakers was produced by grinding grain between great millstones. In windmills, the wind power was used to turn millstones. In watermills, flowing water powered a waterwheel, which provided the turning power. Mills were also used to press olives and to crush seeds to make oil.

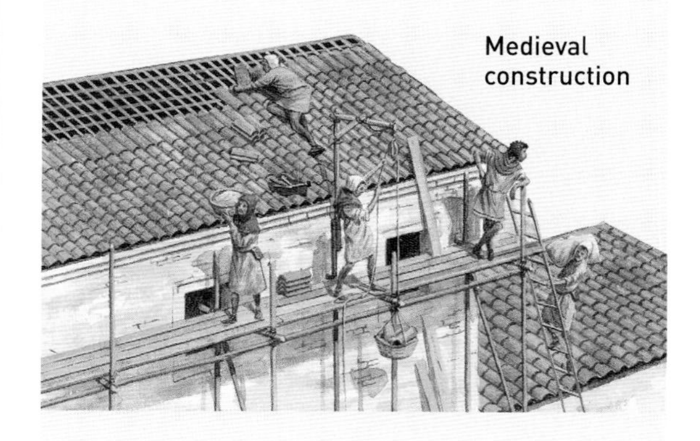

Medieval construction

Shipping: European merchant ships were small and clumsy, with square sails. They traded mostly in coastal waters. Later, Europeans adopted rudders and triangular sails from the Arabs and Chinese. Then they could make great ocean voyages.

Tiles: In southern Europe, roofs were made of pottery tiles. They were less of a fire hazard than the thatched roofs of northern Europe.

17th century

Lenses: Curved pieces of glass used in microscopes, which made small objects look bigger, and telescopes, which made distant objects look nearer.

Scientist with a telescope

Muskets: Guns that needed to be rested on a support to be fired. They took a long time to load. The gunpowder was set off by a shower of sparks.

Springs: Well-made metal springs had an impact on the way devices were made in the 1600s. Small springs were used in making better clocks and guns. Big metal springs were used in building horse-drawn coaches. The springs cushioned passengers against bumps in the road.

Weather instruments: New instruments were invented to measure different kinds of weather. The thermometer measured temperature and the barometer measured air pressure. When air pressure is high, the weather is fine. Barometers helped people forecast the weather. The first weather stations kept daily records from the 1650s.

19th century

Aircraft: Balloons carried the first air passengers in the 1780s. The first powered airships were flown in 1852.

Bicycles: The first bicycle was built in 1839. Air-filled rubber tyres appeared in 1888.

Cars: Petrol-driven cars were invented in Germany in 1885. Within 30 years, new streets and roads were built, traffic lights and speed limits were introduced, and exhaust fumes polluted the air.

Steamships: Iron ships driven by propellers date from 1843. Steamships allowed reliable, fast travel across the ocean.

Street lighting: Gas street lights appeared in Europe in 1814. The first street with permanent electric lighting was in the French city of Lyon, in 1857.

Telephones: Exchanges were opening in European cities by 1879, changing the way people did business and enjoyed themselves.

A street with gas street light and a bicycle

Today

CCTV: Closed-circuit television (CCTV) cameras operate in city centres. They record traffic movements and any crimes or accidents that may occur on the streets.

Computers: Offices began to use big computers in the 1950s. The first personal computers appeared in 1975. The international computer network known as the Internet began in 1987.

Computers

Mobile telephones: The first service started in the USA in 1984. Since the 1990s, mobiles have changed the way people communicate.

Plastics: Cheap, light, artificial materials that can be moulded into any shape. They are used to make packaging, clothing, spectacles, furniture, and countless everyday objects.

Pre-stressed concrete: Used in skyscrapers, bridges, and flyovers, this material is set around tense steel wires for extra strength.

WORK AND PLAY THROUGH TIME

Greek

Drama: The first Greek plays were performed as part of religious festivals. Only men were allowed to act. They wore masks that showed characters or feelings.

Games: Athletics contests held in honour of the gods. Events included running, wrestling, throwing the discus, and chariot racing. Winners received prizes and glory in their home town.

Philosophy: Philosophers tried to answer questions about the world in a scientific way. They also discussed questions of right and wrong.

Politics: The study and practice of government. The word comes from the Greek for city, "polis". Some cities were ruled by kings, some by assemblies of citizens.

Slavery: Greek society relied on slaves to do the hard work without pay.

Warfare: Male citizens served in the army for part of the year and during wartime.

Slaves serving at a banquet

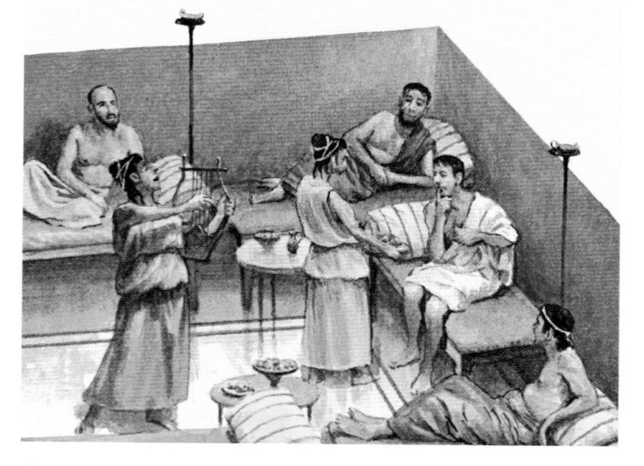

Roman

Army: The army was organized into 28 legions, which were groups of 5,500 professional soldiers. The soldiers had to be Roman citizens.

Boardgames: The Romans liked to play boardgames and to gamble with dice.

Bread supply: Cities imported grain each year to feed their citizens. Donkeys turned millstones, which ground the grain into flour. Loaves were baked in big ovens and some were given to poor people at public expense.

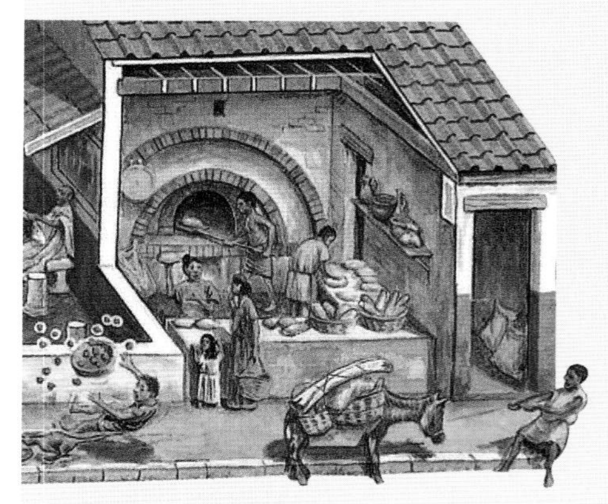

Bakery

Chariot racing: Four horses normally pulled each chariot. Winners could make a fortune in prize money.

Farming: Many retired soldiers owned small farms outside the city walls. Most farms had vegetable plots, fruit trees, and beehives. Richer people owned country estates with larger farms and orchards.

Medicine: Roman doctors knew little science. However, some of their herbal potions worked, and surgeons knew how to mend bones.

Medieval

Knights: Horseback soldiers who became powerful in the Middle Ages. They took oaths of loyalty to a lord and had to serve him when called upon. They were supposed to follow a code of honour.

Pilgrimage: A journey to a sacred place made for religious reasons. Pilgrims travelled across Europe to pray at famous shrines or churches. They wore badges to show where they had been.

Players: Travelling actors who performed plays from wagons or on the steps of cathedrals. The plays were about the lives of saints or events in the Bible. They featured comic scenes and special effects.

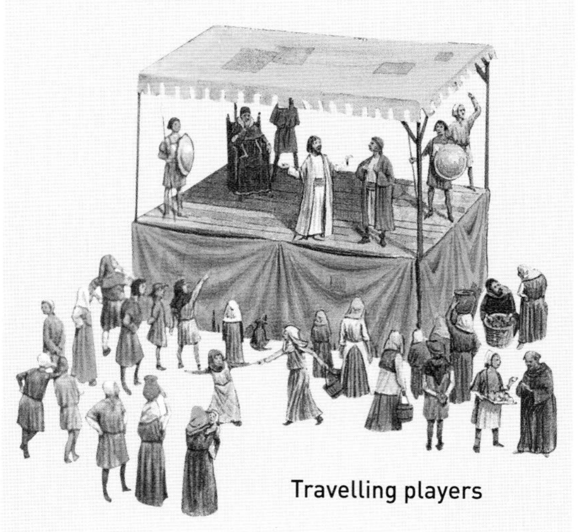

Travelling players

Troubadours: Poets and musicians in southern Europe who wandered from castle to castle. They would praise the local ruler and sing of love.

Weight masters: Officials who watched market traders to make sure they did not cheat by selling under-weight goods.

17th century

Actresses: Women could now act on stage in many countries. They became popular, like today's pop stars.

Courtiers: Nobles who spent most of their time in the royal court. They hoped to gain favours from the king.

Guards: Men with muskets or pikes who formed companies to protect important people or to keep order in cities.

Printing press

Printing: Printing presses were now common in Europe. They replaced scribes who copied books by hand. Presses turned out pamphlets and books. If these criticized the king or the church, the printer was thrown into jail.

Science: Scientists studied the stars. Doctors discovered how the human body works. Some science was still mixed up with superstition. Alchemists tried to find out how to make gold and how to live forever.

Tax collectors: Officials told by the king to collect taxes. They often took much of the money for themselves and became very wealthy.

19th century

Bargees: Men who sailed barges along the rivers and canals of Europe. Barges were like the lorries of their day, transporting industrial goods.

Factory workers: People poured into cities in search of work in factories. Work was poorly paid, dangerous, and unhealthy. Many campaigned for better working conditions.

Industrialists: Factory owners who bought and sold shares in companies. Some became so rich that they never had to work.

Lamp lighting: Gas lamps in city streets had to be lit one by one at nightfall.

Popular songs: Songs that became well known by being played in music halls, opera houses, and dance halls. Families sang them at home, at the piano.

Opera house

Sports: Cycling, rowing, lawn tennis, gymnastics, archery, football, boxing, and billiards all became popular across Europe during this period.

Today

Jogging: Many people like to go for a jog in the park before they go to work, or at lunchtime. It keeps them fit.

Office workers: Workers who sit at desks, use computers and calculators, and talk to clients on the telephone.

Road transport: Lorries take goods right across Europe by road. The containers in the back are all the same size, so they can stack neatly.

Road transport

Sports stadium: Thousands of people gather at stadiums to watch sports. Some of the biggest are built for the Olympic Games, which are held every four years.

Television: Most homes have televisions, which pick up programmes with a cable or a satellite dish. Televisions show news, game shows, drama, music, and sports.

Traffic wardens: If you park in the wrong place, a traffic warden may give you a parking ticket. You may have to pay a fine, or have your car clamped or towed away.

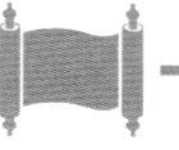

COSTUME THROUGH TIME

Greek

Armour: Soldiers shielded their head and cheeks with crested bronze helmets. They wore a solid bronze cuirass – a combined back- and breast-plate. Bronze greaves (shin guards) protected their legs.

Chiton: A long linen tunic worn by men and women. It was joined over the shoulders and so needed no fastenings.

Hairstyles: Women wore their hair long, often in ringlets. Some tied their hair with nets or ribbons. Men wore their hair short and curled.

Headwear: Some women covered their heads with veils or cloaks. Men went bare-headed, but sometimes wore pointed woollen caps or straw sunhats with big brims.

Peplos: A woman's long woollen dress. It was gathered at the waist and fastened at the shoulder with brooches.

Sandals: Both women and men wore sandals made of leather. Men sometimes wore boots.

Greek soldiers in bronze armour

Roman

Armour: Soldiers wore upper body armour of overlapping bronze plates, which were strapped together, or a mail shirt of interlaced iron rings.

Armour Toga

Cosmetics: Women liked to wear make-up. Powder was made from chalk and eye shadow from ash. Lipstick was made from red ochre (clay) or wine dregs.

Palla: A long shawl worn by women and draped around the head and shoulders.

Stola: A long dress worn by women over an under-tunic.

Toga: A white robe of heavy wool. It was the formal wear of important men. The most important men wore togas with a purple border.

Working dress: Workers and slaves wore simple woollen or linen tunics, which allowed them to move freely.

Wreath: A crown of laurel leaves worn on the head of emperors, successful athletes at the games, and soldiers honoured for their bravery.

Medieval

Armour: Knights wore tunics and leggings made of chain mail. Soon knights began to strap metal plates over their mail for extra protection. On top, they wore a light tunic called a surcoat.

Crowns: Kings wore crowns as badges of royalty. Other royal symbols included rings, gloves, cloaks, swords, and staffs called sceptres.

Hose: Linen or wool leg coverings, rather like tights. They were tucked into pointed boots or shoes of soft leather.

Religious dress: Priests wore long robes. Bishops wore pointed hats called mitres. Monks shaved their heads. Each order of monks had its own dress, or habit.

Knights in armour and surcoats

Tunic: A loose, sleeveless top, usually reaching the knees or the mid-thighs. In the year 1250, men's and women's dress was based upon a tunic design. Noblemen, merchants, and lawyers wore a long costume, while working men wore a short costume, which was more practical.

17th century

Breeches: Short trousers fastened just below the knee. They were fashionable for men from about 1520 until full-length trousers became more popular during the 1800s.

Children's dress: Babies were tightly bound in bands called swaddling clothes until they were six weeks old. Boys and girls then wore pinafores (long dresses). Boys started to wear breeches at six years old.

Fans: In southern Europe, fashionable ladies carried beautiful fans made of silk or ivory to keep themselves cool in the heat of summer.

Military dress: Most soldiers wore only a breastplate and helmet over their normal clothes. Uniforms were beginning to be worn by the 1660s and 1670s.

Petticoats: In the early 1600s, full skirts were draped over hoops worn around a woman's waist. In the 1650s, these were replaced by stiff petticoats.

Wigs: In the late 1600s, men and women took to wearing curled wigs, even if their hair was still in good condition.

17th-century fashion

19th century

Cotton: A material imported to Europe in the 1800s and woven into cloth at large, industrial textile mills.

Dressed for a stroll

Dresses: Crinolines (full-skirted women's petticoats) were in fashion in the 1850s. In the 1880s, women wore narrower skirts with a bustle (a pad or frame inside the skirt) at the bottom.

Footwear: Shoes and ankle-length and knee-length boots were made of polished leather with buttons as fasteners.

Hats: Men wore top hats (tall black hats with a narrow brim). Women wore bonnets decorated with ribbons.

Trousers: In the 1800s, men began to wear trousers rather than breeches and stockings.

Uniforms: Soldiers wore smart uniforms in bright colours. Police forces wore uniforms, as did firemen, nurses, school children, and orphans.

Waterproofs: Waterproof clothes were made from cloth and rubber in the 1830s. The inventor's name, Macintosh, was given to all raincoats.

Today

Jeans: Heavy cotton trousers that were first made for workers in the USA in the 1870s. They are now worn by ordinary men and women around the world. The name "jeans" comes from the Italian city of Genoa, which produced the cloth.

Sportswear: Special fibres and clothes are worn for many sports. Some clothes are worn every day, such as trainers, baseball hats, or football strips.

Suit: A matching jacket and trousers for men, or a matching jacket and skirt or trousers for women. It is formal wear for business or smart occasions, often worn with a shirt and tie.

Sunglasses: Dark glasses were invented in 1885 and remain fashionable today.

Synthetic fibres: Man-made clothing fibres, such as nylon or Lycra®.

T-shirts: Cotton shirts with short sleeves worn by men and women. Many are printed with designs or slogans.

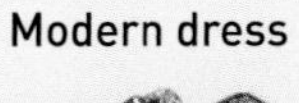

Modern dress

HISTORICAL CITIES

While our city was expanding on the Mediterranean coast in Europe, other urban centres were developing all over the globe. The first cities appeared in the Middle East and the biggest one today is in Asia. Here are some of the greatest cities in the history of the world. Some were capitals of powerful civilizations, whereas others were centres for trade, culture, and learning.

Ur (c. 2000 BCE)

From about 4300 to 3100 BCE, the towns of Sumer in southern Mesopotamia (modern-day Iraq) grew into the world's first cities. One of these was the city of Ur, an important trading port on the Persian gulf. It became very wealthy and was filled with impressive town-houses, lavish palaces, and a huge central mud-brick temple. By about 2000 BCE, Ur was the largest city in the world. It used the world's earliest writing system, called cuneiform, consisting of hundreds of different symbols.

Cuneiform was written on clay tablets

Pharaoh Rameses II built many statues of himself at Thebes

Thebes (c. 1500 BCE)

Sitting on the River Nile, the city of Thebes was capital of Ancient Egypt when the Egyptian empire was at its height. It was named "Thebes" by the Greeks, but to the Egyptians it was known as Waset. On the east bank of the river there were massive temple complexes, which were kilometres wide. Giant statues, obelisks, sphinxes, and columns were built by the pharoahs to honour the gods. The west side of the river was used to bury royalty in elaborate underground tombs.

Athens (c. 450 BCE)

Athens was the largest and most influential of the Ancient Greek city-states. It was named after the Greek goddess Athena. A temple – the Parthenon – was built in her honour. Athens was involved in many wars and had a huge navy. However, it was also a great centre of learning and introduced the world's first system of democracy in the 6th century BCE.

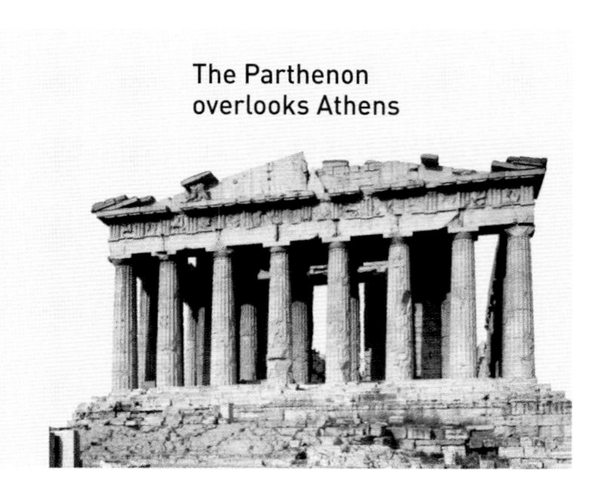

The Parthenon overlooks Athens

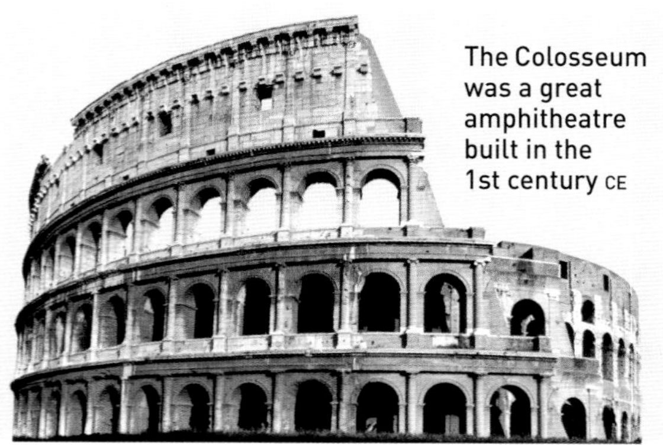

The Colosseum was a great amphitheatre built in the 1st century CE

Rome (c. 100 CE)

According to legend, the city of Rome was founded in 753 BCE. In 509 BCE, Rome became a republic and was ruled by elected officials. The city expanded its territory and by the 1st century CE, Rome was capital of an empire stretching across most of western and southern Europe, North Africa, and the Middle East. Ruled by an emperor, Rome was now the largest and richest city in the world. The emperors filled the city with magnificent public buildings.

The Tikal Temple I is 47 m (154 ft) high

Tikal (c. 200)

Tikal was a capital city in the ancient Maya civilization (in modern-day Guatemala). From 200 CE to 900 CE, it was one of the most important cities in the Maya region, politically, economically, and culturally. During its peak, it was filled with grand palaces and temples. However, the city was often at war, and when it was defeated many of its monuments were burned down. By the 10th century CE, the city was more or less abandoned.

Constantinople (c. 550)

In 476 CE the western Roman empire fell. The eastern half became the Byzantine empire and was ruled from the great city of Constantinople (modern-day Istanbul). The city sat along the trade route to Asia and became very rich. At its heart was the Hagia Sophia, the world's largest church, built by Justinian I in 532 CE.

A mosaic of the Byzantine emperor Justinian I

Chinese art and design flourished in Chang'an during the Tang Dynasty

Chang'an (c. 750)

Chang'an was one of the old capitals of China. During the Tang Dynasty, Chang'an was a centre for Chinese art and culture. It was also at the start of the silk road trade route to Europe. By 750 CE it was one of the largest and most populous cities in the world. The city was surrounded by huge 5-m (18-ft) high city walls, and had beautiful monasteries, pagodas, and shrines.

Baghdad (c. 900)

Baghdad was founded in the 8th century CE and became the capital of the Islamic Abbasid empire. The city was an important intellectual centre and had numerous academic institutions. Scholars gathered here to translate Ancient Greek scientific and philosophical texts into Arabic. The city had an unusual circular design and so was called the "round city". In the centre was a mosque and the great Golden Gate Palace, where the ruler and his family lived.

Islamic texts were often beautifully decorated

Humayun's Tomb in Delhi is an example of Mughal architecture

Delhi (c. 1550)

The city of Delhi is one of the oldest inhabited cities in the world. It has been the capital of numerous empires and been invaded, destroyed, and rebuilt many times. In 1526, Delhi became the capital of the Mughal Empire. The capital was moved to Agra in 1606, but was returned to Delhi in 1648 by the emperor Shah Jahan, who rebuilt the city once more.

London (c. 1850)

London was the largest city in the world from 1831 to 1925. During the early 19th century, it was overcrowded, dirty, and full of disease. Traffic congestion led to the creation of the world's first local urban rail network, linking the city to growing suburbs. In 1863 the world's first underground railway was opened in London. The wealth generated by the Industrial Revolution led to improved public health schemes in the city and the building of grand monuments.

The Palace of Westminster was built from 1840 to 1870

New York (c. 1950)

New York became a single city in 1898 – before then it was a cluster of smaller boroughs. It was a magnet for immigrants and, by the 1920s, New York was the most populous city in the world. The economic boom in the 1920s also funded the construction of several skyscrapers. Finished in 1931, the Empire State Building was the tallest building in the world for 40 years. In the 1950s, when European cities were recovering from World War II, New York became a world centre for finance, art, and media.

The Empire State Building is 381 m (1,250 ft) high

Bullet trains whizz commuters into the city

Tokyo (c. 2000)

Tokyo was almost completely rebuilt after World War II. High-rise developments shot up and the population boomed. By the 21st century, Tokyo had become the world's most populous city and a major economic centre. More than 10 million people commute into the city on a sophisticated travel network. Bullet trains speed in from the suburbs at 580 km/h (360 mph).

INDEX

CREDITS

DK would like to thank:
Philip Steele for the original text, Matilda Gollon for additional text, Philip Parker for historical consultancy, and Jenny Sich for proofreading.

The Publisher would like to thank the following for their kind permission to reproduce their photographs:

a=above, c=centre, b=below, l=left, r=right, t=top

42 Getty Images: De Agostini (crb); Adam Woolfitt / Robert Harding (bl). **43 Corbis:** Danny Lehman (tl). **Getty Images:** Dea / A. De Gregorio (cr); Chinese School (clb); Dea / J. E. Bulloz (br). **44 Corbis:** Andrea Jemolo (r). **Getty Images:** Danita Delimont (t); Rory Gordon - Michael Ramage (bl)

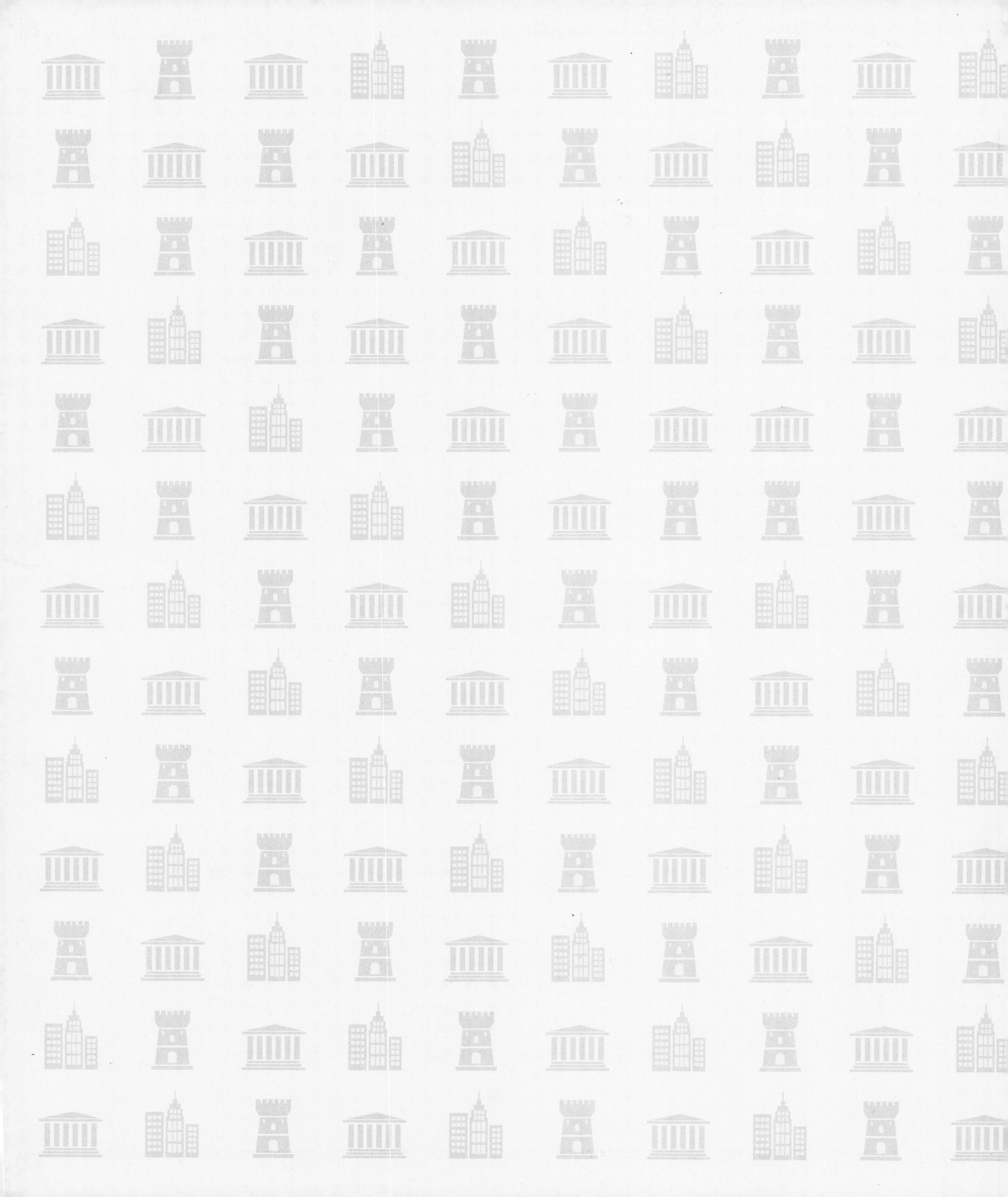